All About
Hurricanes

Ann McCallum Staats, M.Ed.

Consultants

Dr. Aaron O'Dea,
Dr. Erin Dillon, Dr. Natasha Hinojosa,
and Dr. Kimberly García-Méndez
Researchers
Smithsonian Tropical Research Institute

Cheryl Lane, M.Ed.
Seventh Grade Science Teacher
Chino Valley Unified School District

Michelle Wertman, M.S.Ed.
Literacy Specialist
New York City Public Schools

Publishing Credits

Rachelle Cracchiolo, M.S.Ed., *Publisher*
Emily R. Smith, M.A.Ed., *SVP of Content Development*
Véronique Bos, *VP of Creative*
Dani Neiley, *Editor*
Fabiola Sepulveda, *Art Director*

Smithsonian Enterprises

Avery Naughton, *Licensing Coordinator*
Paige Towler, *Editorial Lead*
Jill Corcoran, *Senior Director, Licensed Publishing*
Brigid Ferraro, *Vice President of New Business and Licensing*
Carol LeBlanc, *President*

Image Credits: p.5 Mr. and Mrs. Martin A. Ryerson Collection/
Bridgeman Images; p.13 NOAA, Office for Coastal Management,
DigitalCoast; p.14 Alamy Stock Photo/Operation 2022;
p.15 (top) APFootage/Alamy Stock Photo; p.15 (bottom) Staff Sgt. Randy
Redman of the US Air Force; p.17 Library of Congress [LC-2021669944];
p.20 (top) Library of Congress [LC-USW3- 038389-D [P&P] LOT 910];
p.20 (bottom) Alamy/Jeffrey Isaac Greenberg 7+; p.26, 32 Getty Images/
Joe Raedle/Staff; all other images from iStock and/or Shutterstock
or in the public domain

Library of Congress Cataloging in Publication Control Number:
2024039527

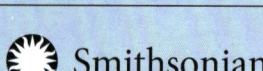

TCM Teacher Created Materials

5482 Argosy Avenue
Huntington Beach, CA 92649
www.tcmpub.com
ISBN 979-8-7659-6895-6
© 2025 Teacher Created Materials, Inc.
Printed by: 51497
Printed in: China

Table of Contents

Bad Weather Ahead

As all sailors know, storms pop up often over the oceans. Storms can bring rain, lightning, thunder, and strong winds. Some storms become dangerous and powerful quickly. When an organized system of clouds and thunderstorms forms over a low pressure area and begins rotating over tropical waters, it is known as a tropical depression. This type of storm is relatively minor and does not cause a lot of damage. If the winds pick up and a depression becomes stronger, it becomes a tropical storm. And if a tropical storm builds up even stronger winds, it expands into its most powerful form—a hurricane.

Hurricanes form over warm ocean water. They can cause massive destruction if they make **landfall**. For a storm to be categorized as a hurricane, its winds have to travel at least 119 kilometers (74 miles) per hour.

This satellite photo shows the characteristic spiral shape of a hurricane as it approaches land.

Strong winds affect palm trees during a typhoon in Thailand.

Depending on where you are in the world, this weather event goes by a different name. It's a hurricane if it starts in the northern Atlantic or northeast Pacific Oceans. It's a tropical cyclone in the Indian or South Pacific Oceans. In the northwest Pacific, people refer to it as a typhoon. In this book, we'll use the term *hurricane*.

Wherever hurricanes happen, they bring heavy rain and strong winds. These storms can cause extensive damage and flooding. Learning how these storms form, how experts categorize them, and what technology they use to study them can help us better prepare for them.

Taking Art by Storm

Throughout history, people have created art to show the power of storms. Winslow Homer painted "After the Hurricane" in 1899. This watercolor painting reminds us how dangerous these weather events can be.

Climate Versus Weather

Before learning all about hurricanes, it's important to know the difference between weather and climate. Here's an easy definition: weather is the current state of Earth's atmosphere. It changes every day. Meanwhile, climate is the average weather conditions of an area over time.

Climate refers to typical, long-term trends during yearly seasons. Many different factors affect climate. A place's distance from the **equator** and its **altitude** affect climate. Features including mountains or lakes can affect climate, too. **Meteorologists** gather climate data. They look at the weather in an area for the past 30 years. They can calculate the average temperatures that occurred every month and determine average patterns of weather. For example, they might see that a place gets rain and cold temperatures in March. This information helps them determine the overall climate.

Climate tells you what types of clothes to have in your closet.

Weather tells you what to wear each day.

When it comes to weather, it tends to change every day. People can check the weather forecast to know if it's a day for shorts and a T-shirt or a warm jacket and gloves. Forecasts provide short-term information on hourly, daily, or weekly weather conditions. Weather involves temperature, wind, sunshine, **humidity**, or cloud cover. It also includes **precipitation**, which may be rain, hail, snow, or sleet.

The Pressure's On

When you think of wind, various words may come to mind. These might include breeze, gust, or draft. Or it may include different kinds of wind, such as **zephyr** and **chinook**. Wind can be mild or, during a hurricane, exceptionally powerful. But what is wind? How does it form, and how does it build?

Wind is the movement of air. Air is made of molecules, which are groups of atoms chemically bonded together. These molecules are made of different elements, including nitrogen, oxygen, and small amounts of carbon dioxide.

SCIENCE

Let's Go Fly a Kite

Kites stay up in the sky because of the air pushing against them. If there is enough wind and the kite is angled the right way, it receives *lift*. The kite goes up and up, defying gravity. At the same time, a resistant force called *drag* acts on the kite. It tries to pull it back toward the ground. But if there is more lift than drag, the kite can stay balanced in the sky.

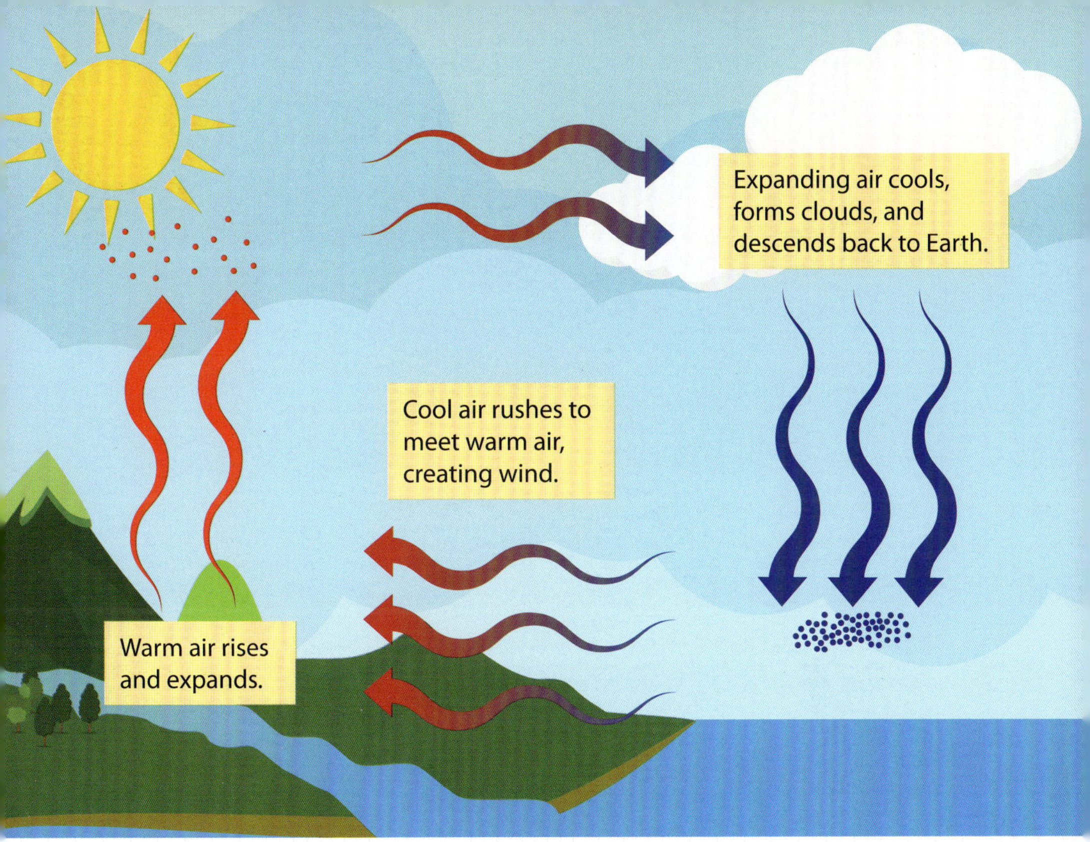

Expanding air cools, forms clouds, and descends back to Earth.

Cool air rushes to meet warm air, creating wind.

Warm air rises and expands.

Wind is caused by changes in temperatures of air, land, and water. As the sun heats parts of Earth, air is warmed. This air rises. And when air increases in temperature, the molecules become less dense. This means there is less pressure. Meanwhile, cold air is the opposite. With colder air, molecules squeeze close together as more molecules fill the same space. This density creates a pocket of high pressure. As cool, high-pressure air meets an area of low pressure, the cooler air rushes in to fill in the extra space. This rushing of air is wind.

During hurricanes, powerful winds occur. That's because the greater the difference in air pressure, the faster the wind blows.

picks up moisture, which **evaporates** as it rises. When the water vapor cools, it creates clouds. These clouds grow into a swirling storm system. The whole process can take up to a week for a hurricane to form.

HURRICANE FORMATION

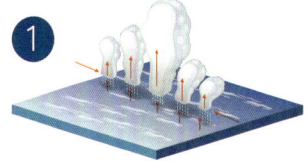

Warm, rising air condenses and begins to form storm clouds.

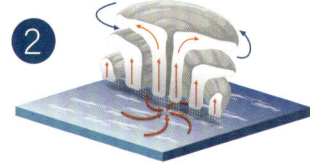

Warm ocean water continues to fuel the storm system. Heavy rains and strong winds occur. A feedback loop is created as cool air is pushed out of the top of the storm system, is warmed as it descends, and is pulled back in at the bottom.

More rising air begins to build up a storm system with rain and wind. Earth's rotation causes the entire system to spin.

A hurricane has different parts. In its center is the eye. This is a circular area of calm, clear air that is 32–64 km (20–40 mi.) wide. Surrounding the eye is the eyewall. Here, you'll find the storm's most violent wind and intense rain. Farther out, bands of rain spread out until the entire hurricane is an average of 483 km (300 mi.) wide.

When a hurricane reaches land, its rain and strong winds typically last up to 24 hours. In rare cases, strong winds may last for 48 hours. But all hurricanes eventually **dissipate**. Over land, wind ends up slowing and changing direction. Without the warm ocean water and air supply to fuel hurricanes, they lose their power and fade.

FUN FACT

The largest hurricane on record began near the Philippines in 1979. Typhoon Tip measured 2,219 km (1,379 mi.) in diameter. It caused major devastation when it struck Japan.

Going in Circles

When hurricanes form, they have recognizable spiral patterns. And as they travel across the ocean toward land, they keep their spiral shapes. This is where the **Coriolis Effect** comes in. In 1835, Gaspard Gustave de Coriolis was the first person to name this interesting phenomenon.

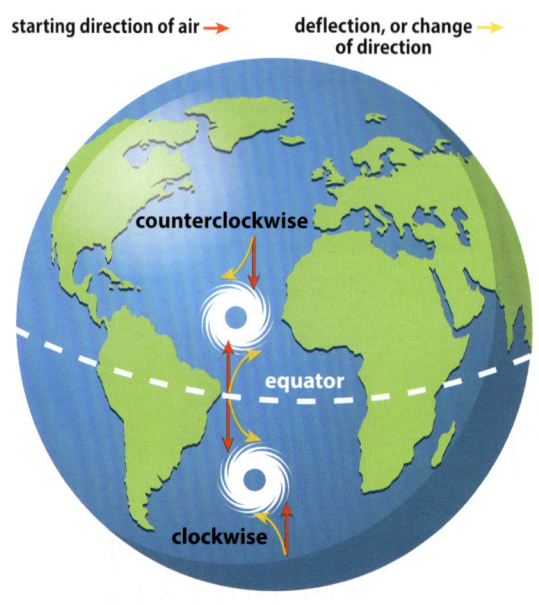

starting direction of air →   deflection, or change → of direction

counterclockwise

equator

clockwise

In a hurricane, this effect causes the circulating pattern of air. Remember that intense wind forms when high-pressure air swoops into an area of low pressure. In other words, colder air rushes into pockets of warmer air where there is more room. When a hurricane is north of the equator, its winds spin in a counterclockwise direction. South of the equator, hurricane winds turn clockwise. All the while, Earth is rotating on its axis. Every 24 hours, Earth makes one complete turn. So, as hurricanes move across oceans, their paths appear to curve. Because of the Coriolis Effect, something that moves in a straight line looks curved because Earth is constantly moving.

Here's an example to visualize. Imagine throwing a baseball from a rotating carousel. You throw the ball straight ahead of you, but the ball lands somewhere past where you were aiming. The turning of the carousel has moved the ball farther to the right or left, depending on the direction the deck is turning. The Coriolis Effect affects hurricanes the same way as they travel across water.

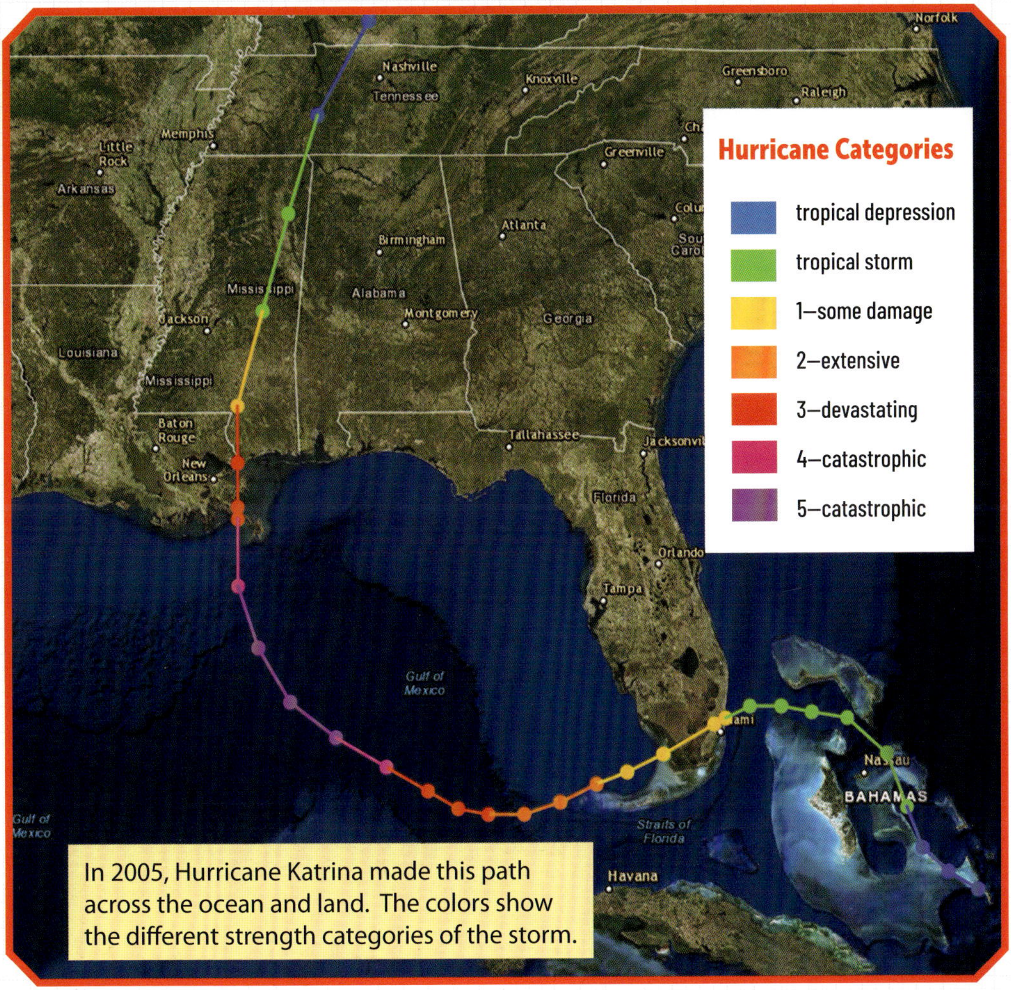

Hurricane Categories

![blue]	tropical depression
![green]	tropical storm
![yellow]	1—some damage
![orange]	2—extensive
![red]	3—devastating
![pink]	4—catastrophic
![purple]	5—catastrophic

In 2005, Hurricane Katrina made this path across the ocean and land. The colors show the different strength categories of the storm.

FUN FACT

Hurricanes cannot form near the equator. You will never see a hurricane form within 483 km (300 mi.) of the equator. That's because Earth's spin is very slow there. This means the Coriolis Effect is weak. Hurricanes need quickly rotating air to develop.

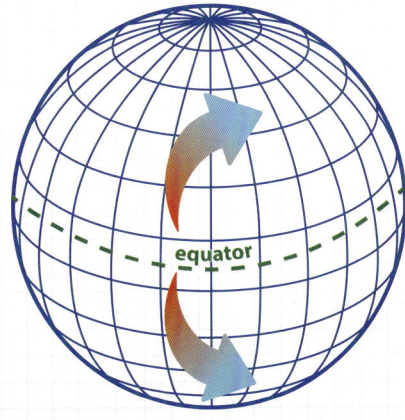

Keeping Track

To prepare for hurricanes, scientists gather as much data as they can. The more scientists know, the more accurate their warnings will be for the people in the path of a hurricane.

Before the 1960s, scientists tried to predict when and where hurricanes would occur. However, there were a lot of surprises. Their jobs got easier with the invention of satellites. From space, satellites take pictures and record measurements to send to Earth. In the United States today, certain satellites are positioned over the East and West coasts. These satellites send storm and weather data to Earth every 30 seconds or so. This way, scientists can easily spot the first signs of a tropical depression. They can closely monitor an area to see whether the depression will develop into a hurricane.

A crew of hurricane hunters gives a briefing on a hurricane.

This hurricane hunter plane is used to fly through hurricanes.

Monitoring storms from above Earth isn't the only way to keep track of hurricanes. There are also specially designed aircraft nicknamed "hurricane hunters." These planes are built to withstand dangerous hurricane conditions. They can fly back and forth through hurricanes, collecting data. Their crews include pilots, engineers, and other scientists. Their missions are usually several hours long. Onboard are computers, **radar**, and weather instruments. This technology pinpoints the strength of a storm. It can also predict the storm's path and timing. This is helpful because if the hurricane is projected to hit land, residents need maximum time to prepare or **evacuate**.

TECHNOLOGY

Dropping In

A **dropsonde** is used to measure hurricane data. This tool is dropped from an aircraft during a hurricane. The small device is attached to a mini-parachute. It records air pressure, temperature, and humidity as it falls to the ocean.

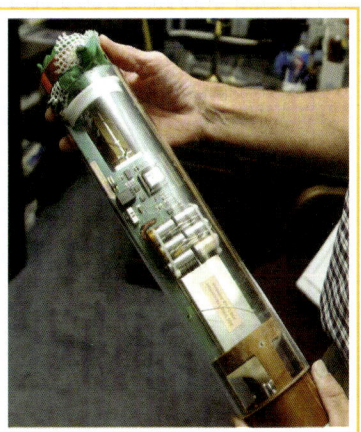

Measuring Up

Before the 1970s, people had no way of measuring how severe a hurricane was. Then, an engineer and a meteorologist developed a scale of intensity. Herbert Saffir and Bob Simpson came up with a system called the *Saffir-Simpson Scale*. This scale is based on wind speed. Today, scientists use this scale to estimate the potential damage of hurricanes.

The scale has five levels. The first is Category 1. At this level, wind speeds range from 119–153 km (74–95 mi.) per hour. These dangerous winds race by faster than some cars on a highway. Buildings and trees may be damaged. Unanchored objects, such as umbrellas or pool chairs, may fly through the air. Category 2 hurricanes have even faster winds up to 177 km (110 mi.) per hour. At this level, there is more extensive damage to buildings. Trees may be uprooted, and power outages are almost certain.

Categories 3, 4, and 5 mark major hurricanes. These storms are extremely destructive. Windows can shatter, and many buildings may be flattened. It can take weeks or months for power to be restored and buildings to be repaired. If wind speeds are above 252 km (157 mi.) per hour, the hurricane is a Category 5. Damage is so **catastrophic** that things may never be the same after it. Loss of life is almost certain.

Category	Wind Speed (per hour)	Damage Level
1	119–153 km (74–95 mi.)	some
2	154–177 km (96–110 mi.)	extensive
3	178–208 km (111–129 mi.)	devastating
4	209–251 km (130–156 mi.)	catastrophic
5	252 km and above (157 mi.)	catastrophic

Hurricane Ian flooded neighborhoods in Florida in 2022.

Strong winds that occur in hurricanes can tear homes and other buildings apart.

Storm Surges

Strong winds aren't the only deadly forces in hurricanes. Storm surges happen when extra water causes the ocean to rise above the normal **tide** level. These surges can be up to 6 meters (20 feet) above normal! Scientists can feed data on a hurricane into a computer to make predictions about the expected storm surge.

What's in a Name?

When you meet someone new, you'll likely ask for their name. Their name helps you identify the person. The same is true for hurricanes—they all have names! Naming hurricanes allows weather experts to communicate with ships and weather stations scattered around the world. Plus, specific names are useful when multiple storms occur at once.

FUN FACT

When a hurricane is especially devastating, its name is retired. It won't be used again for future storms. A new name is added to the list to replace it.

Retired Atlantic Hurricane Names

Agnes	1972
Alicia	1983
Allen	1980
Allison	2001
Andrew	1992
Anita	1977
Audrey	1957

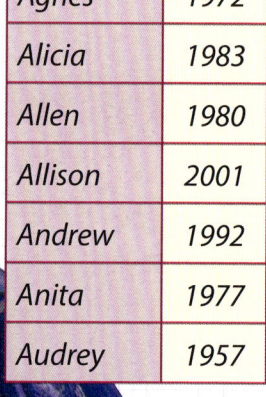

A weather satellite took this photo of Hurricane Andrew making landfall in 1992.

Throughout history, when significant storms hit, people labeled them. For example, in the **West Indies**, early storms were given religious names. Each day of the year was associated with a saint. So, when a hurricane hit Puerto Rico on September 13, 1876, it was named after San Felipe. This method became confusing when storms landed on the same day in different years. When another hurricane hit on September 13, 1928, it was called San Felipe II.

During World War II, scientists in the United States tried a new naming method. They used names in alphabetical order that were based on radio codes. Able, Baker, and Charlie were some of the names. Then, in 1953, the U.S. National Hurricane Center started using women's names. By 1979, lists included both men's and women's names.

Today, the World Meteorological Organization is in charge of naming hurricanes. They make lists of easy-to-pronounce names that can be assigned to significant storms. For hurricanes in the Atlantic Ocean, there are six different name lists that are reused every six years.

Tropical storm Allison caused significant flood damage in Texas in 2001. As a result, its name was retired.

Hurricane Incoming!

During hurricane season, the biggest question is whether a hurricane will reach land. In the United States, experts at the National Hurricane Center are in charge of alerting people. They use a system to tell people of the chances that a hurricane will strike their area. There are two different alerts.

These tools at the U.S. Weather Bureau Station in 1943 monitored weather conditions.

At first, experts release a hurricane watch. A watch means that it's possible that a hurricane could affect a region within the next 48 hours. Just in case, residents should start to prepare. Experts continue to monitor the storm as it develops.

Experts at the National Hurricane Center track a hurricane.

When experts release a hurricane warning, it means that a hurricane is expected. Experts are certain that a hurricane will arrive within the next 36 hours. Depending on how strong it's expected to be, people might be asked to evacuate. If so, those who live in the hurricane's path should pack their essential belongings and leave their homes immediately. They will be directed to an area that is a safe distance from the storm. Temporary shelters may be set up for people who need them.

Sometimes, evacuations aren't necessary for a hurricane. But there are still plenty of things to do to prepare. Because of the high wind danger, people remove any loose furniture or items like bikes and tools from their yards. They might put up wooden boards over glass windows and doors. They might also cut down branches from nearby trees.

ENGINEERING

Built for Wind

Engineers design buildings to withstand the wind from hurricanes. They use strong materials, such as reinforced concrete and steel. They include impact-resistant glass for windows. Also, they avoid creating sharp corners so that wind can flow smoothly past a building rather than flattening it.

Hurricane shutters attach to the walls around doors and windows to protect a building from strong winds.

Hurricane Arrival

When a hurricane hits, it's best to move to an interior room of a building. Glass windows and doors may be blown out, so people should stay far away from them. People should also have a few days' supply of food and water, along with flashlights. Power and water service may be interrupted for days—or longer.

Despite the precautions people take, hurricanes can be deadly. The worst hurricane in U.S. history occurred in 1900 in Texas. It is called the Galveston Hurricane. It claimed over 8,000 lives and destroyed thousands of buildings. One of the worst problems was an enormous storm surge of more than 4.6 m (15 ft.). Strong winds pushed water ashore, flooding the coast and causing many deaths.

The 1900 Galveston Hurricane caused widespread damage across the city.

the aftermath of
Hurricane Katrina

Hurricanes in past decades have not been as deadly. But they have still taken lives and caused billions of dollars in damages. In 2005, Hurricane Katrina resulted in more than 1,800 deaths and over $160 billion in damages. The worst destruction happened in the city of New Orleans, Louisiana. The **floodwalls** surrounding the city failed. Water poured into low-lying areas, trapping people. Then, in 2017, six major hurricanes made landfall in the United States. Three were classified as Category 4 hurricanes. When Hurricane Maria landed in Puerto Rico, it knocked out electricity and water supplies for months. People dealt with the damage and its remaining effects for years afterward.

the aftermath of
Hurricane Maria

Resounding Impacts

Pounding rain. Raging winds. Massive flooding as seawater comes ashore. Wherever hurricanes cross onto land, they **disrupt** life in every way. People may have to leave their homes and can face plenty of hardship—sometimes for months or longer. At times, lives are lost due to falling debris, excessive flooding, and lack of medical care. Animals lose their homes and food supplies, too. After a hurricane, the environment may be completely changed.

A person travels by kayak after a hurricane caused a neighborhood street to flood.

But there's another side to these storms. When they are mild, hurricanes may have some positive effects. For example, hurricanes help balance the temperature throughout the globe. Because the sun heats the world unevenly, the equator is warmer than other places on the planet. It has more direct access to the sun. Meanwhile, the poles are tilted away from the sun. As a result, these areas are much colder. This temperature difference would be much more extreme if it weren't for hurricanes. Hurricanes push warmer air north and south, helping to balance the planet's temperature.

Hurricanes are beneficial in other ways, too. Wind helps spread seeds farther inland, allowing new plants to sprout and grow in other regions. Hurricanes can also bring rain to areas that are dry. They help to end periods of drought. Finally, as hurricanes form, they stir up ocean water beneath them. They bring nutrients up from the bottom of the ocean. This gives fish and other wildlife that live near the surface a healthy food supply.

Hurricane-strength winds spread seeds to new locations, leading to new plant growth.

Weathering the Storm

Whether they are mild or chaotic, hurricanes make themselves known. As they build over warm ocean water, they gain energy and power. When they develop into stronger storms, they can lead to major disruption for anyone—and anything—in their paths.

Hurricanes are more likely to form in certain regions of the world. They occur mostly during hurricane season when conditions are just right. These massive storms need heat and moisture to develop into their signature, swirling masses. They must also have wind that is blowing in the right direction and at the right speed. Scientists track the full life of these storms from beginning to end. They use a variety of satellites and equipment to collect data along the way.

All hurricanes start as storm systems that form over the ocean.

Weather satellites in space track the formation and progress of hurricanes.

Hurricanes, like all natural events, are affected by a changing climate. As the world heats up, more water vapor enters the air. For a hurricane, this provides additional fuel to increase its strength. Also, because of rising sea levels, the height of a storm surge onto land can be more dramatic.

Scientists agree that while it's difficult to predict future weather, it's important to plan ahead. There is no stopping storms. But when people have enough time to prepare, the cost to life and property can be reduced. Experts around the world stay at the ready, continuing to monitor the weather and watching for any incoming hurricanes.

STEAM CHALLENGE

Define the Problem

For people living along the Atlantic coast, hurricanes may be a threat at the conclusion of each summer. Damaging winds and storm surges can severely harm a person's home and belongings. Engineers in these areas have requested ideas for a barrier to help protect homes from wind and water. Your team will need to develop a protective wall that can withstand these two forces of nature.

Constraints: You may only use the materials provided to you.

Criteria: Your protective barrier must fit inside the plastic tray provided to you. It must withstand the force of a fan at different speeds and also keep a home (represented by a coffee filter) dry within the walls when your tray is flooded.

Research and Brainstorm

What are storm surges, and why do they occur? What building materials can withstand the power of Category 3, 4, and 5 winds? How can you keep water out of your model home and thwart high winds?

Design and Build

Sketch a plan that includes a protective barrier surrounding a home. Detail how you plan to create this structure and what materials you will use. Then, meet with your team to share your ideas. Combine your ideas to create one new prototype. Collect the materials needed, and build your barrier wall inside your plastic tray.

Test and Improve

Bring your model to the front of the room. Place a dry coffee filter inside your barrier wall and secure it with a rock. Pour water into your tray on the outside of your wall. Turn on the fan, starting at the lowest speed. Place your model in front of the fan. Increase the speed every 30 seconds until you reach the max speed. Has your wall stopped water from reaching your home? Make improvements to your model and test it again.

Reflect and Share

What aspect of this challenge was most engaging? How did you and your team support one another's ideas? Explain what kinds of variables make hurricane preparations challenging.

Glossary

altitude—the height of an object in relation to sea level, or ground level

catastrophic—involving or causing sudden great damage or suffering

chinook—a warm, westerly wind in western North America

Coriolis Effect—the force that acts on objects in motion, making them appear to move at a curve

disrupt—to throw into disorder

dissipate—to break up and scatter or vanish

dropsonde—a weather instrument dropped from an airplane to measure temperature, pressure, and moisture

equator—imaginary line that divides Earth into the Northern Hemisphere and the Southern Hemisphere

evacuate—leave a place of danger to go to a safer place

evaporates—turns from a liquid into vapor, or gas

floodwalls—walls built to prevent flooding

humidity—the amount of water vapor in the air or atmosphere

landfall—a reaching of land (as by a storm)

meteorologists—scientists who study Earth's atmosphere, weather, and climate

precipitation—water forms, such as rain, sleet, hail, or snow, that fall from clouds

radar—a device that sends out radio waves for finding and locating an object by the reflection of the radio waves

tide—the alternate rising and falling of the sea

West Indies—a geographical area made of 13 island countries, surrounded by the North Atlantic Ocean and the Caribbean Sea

zephyr—a soft and gentle breeze

Index

Do you want to study storms and weather?

Here are some tips to keep in mind for the future.

"Researching about the different ways to predict and prepare for a hurricane is a great way to learn about the practical applications of meteorology."

– Dr. Aaron O'Dea, Staff Scientist, Smithsonian Tropical Research Institute

"Can you predict the path of a hurricane? Online tools are a great way to track each one as it approaches land. Try tracking other storms, too!"

– Dr. Kimberly García-Méndez, Lab Manager, Smithsonian Tropical Research Institute